People at Work

by Joy Darlington

Editorial Offices: Glenview, Illinois • Parsippany, New Jersey • New York, New York
Sales Offices: Needham, Massachusetts • Duluth, Georgia • Glenview, Illinois
Coppell, Texas • Ontario, California • Mesa, Arizona

Come and watch us work. Learn how we do our many different **jobs**.

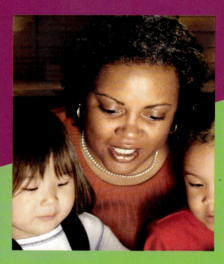

Meet Joe. Joe works in a busy factory. He makes crayons in many different colors.

Meet Emma. Emma runs a daycare center in her home. She takes care of small children.

Meet Maria. She is a plumber. She uses her wrench and other **tools** to fix broken pipes.

Meet Oliver. Oliver works for free. He is a **volunteer** at a hospital. He reads books to patients. He talks with them.

What kind of work would you like to do? Why?

Glossary

jobs the work people do

tools things that are used to help
people do work

volunteer a person who works
for free